A Guide to the A
of South Devon

Paul Rainbird

THREE BARROWS BOOKS

First published in Great Britain 2010

ISBN 978-0-9564991-0-3

Published by Three Barrows Books
Murtwell Barn
Diptford
Devon TQ9 7NQ
England, UK

www.threebarrowsbooks.co.uk

Printed and bound by
Kingfisher Print & Design Ltd
Wills Road
Totnes
Devon TQ9 5XN

Introduction

This guide provides an introduction to the archaeology of South Devon dated to before the Norman invasion of AD 1066. All of the sites in this guide can be located on the 1:50,000 *Ordnance Survey Landranger Map of Torbay and South Dartmoor* (Number 202). In order to aid location national grid references (NGRs) are provided with each site description. For more detailed location, particularly for those sites located on Dartmoor, this guide ought to be used in conjunction with either the *Ordnance Survey Explorer Map of Dartmoor* (Number OL28) or the *Ordnance Survey Explorer Map of South Devon* (Number OL20). All of the sites listed in this guide have been selected with regard to their accessibility, but many are located in rough and exposed terrain and all usual precautions should be taken before making visits. The weather on Dartmoor can become inclement rapidly and map and compass are advisable.

Please do not disturb an archaeological site by moving stones or digging, this may not only destroy vital evidence, but in most cases you are likely to be breaking the law. Although at the time of printing all sites are accessible to the public, please respect the fact that the majority are on private land (even those on the moors) and avoid damaging fences or disturbing livestock and crops, in addition, please respect any temporary restrictions.

An Introduction to Archaeological Periods

The earliest archaeological period is the **Palaeolithic** (Old Stone Age) and includes the earliest evidence for humans in Britain, currently dated to around 700,000 years ago. The Palaeolithic lasts until the end of the last Ice Age, about 10,000 years ago. During this time there were several Ice Ages and people moved in and out of the land now forming Britain as the ice dictated. They survived by gathering plant foods and hunting animals. The landscape of South Devon dramatically altered several times over this period as sea levels changed due to the amount of water trapped in the ice caps. The last Ice Age lasted from about 32,000 years ago until 10,000 years ago when the climate warmed and the sea returned to the valley where the English Channel is today. During the Ice Ages people could walk to Britain from the European continent as it was a peninsula rather than an island. Animals such as Woolly Mammoths and bears also migrated to Britain as the weather allowed and proved vital for the survival of people as sources of food and fur for clothing. Although there are many caves in South Devon with fossil animal remains, such as those at Brixham, Buckfastleigh, Torbryan and Yealmpton, the best evidence for human settlement in this period is derived from Kents Cavern (Site 1). Elsewhere in Devon gravel quarries have yielded fine collections of flint hand axes typical of this period, such as those from Broom, in the appropriately named valley of the River Axe – a selection of these are displayed in the Royal Albert Memorial Museum, Exeter.

Following the end of the last Ice Age people adapted to the new plants and animals that the warmer climate provided. At this time vegetation was being burned on upland areas such as Dartmoor, perhaps creating green shoots to attract wildlife for hunting, but this did not prevent the land of Devon more generally becoming thickly wooded. This period, known as the **Mesolithic** (Middle Stone Age), lasted for approximately 4,000 years up to about 6,000 years ago and in South Devon is represented by scatters of flint tools and stray finds; such finds have been made at the spectacular coastal promontory of Start Point (SX826372). Elsewhere in Britain, such as the Inner Hebrides islands, there is much exploitation of seafood and it is likely that the South Devon coast was being harvested in a similar way.

Fig 1: Start Point

Beginning about 6,000 years ago and lasting until approximately 4,500 years ago is the **Neolithic** (New Stone Age). This period represents a major change from earlier times as people appear to begin to become far more settled in the landscape. Pottery was used for the first time and new types of stone tools, such as polished stone axes, appear. Animals and plants such as sheep, domestic breeds of cattle and wheat and barley are introduced to Britain for the first time. Burial monuments are built, such as chambered tombs, the best known in Devon is at Spinster's Rock north of Chagford (SX701907). In South Devon we have examples at Corringdon Ball and Cuckoo Ball (Sites 2 & 3), and another, a 'passage grave' variant, has been excavated above the beach at Broadsands, Paignton (SX 895573). A further new feature at this time is communal meeting places on hilltops defined by one or more circular circuits of stone or earth with segmented walls and/or ditches, divided by causeways and thus usually termed 'Causewayed Camps' or 'Interrupted

Fig 2: Hazard Hill

Ditch Enclosures', the best known in Devon is at Hembury Hillfort in East Devon on the Blackdown Hills (ST113031), but a likely contender in South Devon is at Hazard Hill west of Totnes (SX755594) where the enclosing circuit is not yet confirmed, but much material of the period has been excavated on the summit. Towards the end of the Neolithic a tradition of building different types of stone and earth monuments began, for example, the rows and circles so typical of Dartmoor and construction of these continued in to the Bronze Age.

The **Bronze Age** begins at approximately 4,500 years ago and continues to about 2,800 years ago. The earlier Bronze Age shows many continuities with the end of the Neolithic, but at this time, apart from the introduction of bronze (an alloy of 90% copper and 10% tin) for tools, there begins the construction of round barrows (piles of earth) and round cairns (piles of stone) for the burial of individuals. Fine examples of round cairns on prominent hill tops are found in the area covered by this guide, particularly on the fringes of Dartmoor, and the cairns at Three Barrows are described (Site 8). Despite the first introduction of domestic animals and plants several centuries earlier it is not until the middle of the Bronze Age that strong evidence of permanent settlement and farming is found in South Devon. Here, Dartmoor has some of the best preserved evidence in Europe, and an example of a settlement of this date is Rider's Rings (site 9). The boundaries defining the field systems are known locally on Dartmoor as reaves and represent the enclosure of huge swathes of the upland edges; reaves can be seen at Saddlesborough (Site 10) and Three Barrows (Site 8). The stone built settlements of Dartmoor appear to continue in use through the later Bronze Age and in to the Iron Age when eventually they are abandoned, perhaps due to a change in the climate to wetter and windier conditions.

The **Iron Age** dates from about 2,800 years ago until the coming of the Romans. In this period objects manufactured from iron are produced and wheel-turned pottery is introduced for the first time. In Southwest England a fine pottery type known formerly as Glastonbury Ware and more recently as Southwest Decorated Ware has curvilinear decoration which shares

5

similarities with the art of the Celts of continental Europe. The major field monument of this period is the hillfort, an enclosure created by one or more bank and ditch. Several are to be found in South Devon and the most accessible are listed in the Guide. These places may have been settlements or refuges in times of danger. Few in South Devon have been excavated, but hillforts elsewhere, such as Danebury in Hampshire and Maiden Castle in Dorset, show that they could be intensively settled with round houses arranged along streets. Another type of site of this period is a variant of the hillfort found in South Wales and Southwest England and is called a 'multiple enclosure hill-slope fort' and appears to be constructed for protected paddocks rather than defence from attack. An excellent example of this type is Milber Down, near Newton Abbot (Site 12). In South Devon, and contemporary with the hillforts, is a landscape of scattered farmsteads consisting of a four-sided bank and ditch enclosure surrounding one or two roundhouses. The remains are usually

Fig 3: Mount Batten

ploughed out and are often only discovered through aerial photography. One site of this type has been extensively excavated at Mount Folly above Bigbury-on-Sea (SX660447). As predicted by the excavator, Eileen Wilkes, the ceramics from Mount Folly show that connections were being made across the English Channel. Further evidence of such contacts has been found on the peninsula of Mount Batten on the south side of the entrance to Cattewater, Plymouth (SX425533) where the excavator, Barry Cunliffe, found a trading port. The former RAF installation is now a residential development where the eminent archaeologist has been commemorated in the naming of 'Cunliffe Avenue'! Remnants of field systems of this period can be found at various locations throughout South Devon, with an easily accessible example at Walls Hill, Babbacombe, Torquay (Site 11).

The arrival of the **Romans** (dates for the Roman occupation of Britain are usually given as AD 43 to 410) led to the demise of hillforts, but the pattern of dispersed farmsteads continued. Roman influence appears to have been very limited in South Devon and west of Exeter the interest in the region appears to be limited to metal ore resources. The Roman road west from Exeter which crosses the Haldon Hills has only been traced as far as the Teign (at Teignbridge) and to date no formal Roman installations are known in South Devon. Roman period finds have been found at the type of farmstead sites that would not be out of place in the Iron Age. One of the best known through excavation is located at Lower Well Farm, near Stoke Gabriel (SX864576) and in favourable conditions the earthworks of the enclosures and fields can be seen from the lane to the southwest.

With the demise of the Romans it appears that South Devon quickly reverted to Iron Age patterns of social organisation and some of the abandoned hillforts may have been re-settled - this is vividly described for the hillfort at Denbury Camp (Site 15) in Derek Gore's historical novel *Isca – The Fall of Roman Exeter*. Trade continued along the south coast and Mediterranean ceramics dating from between the 5th and 8th centuries AD have been found just beyond the beach at Mothecombe and Bantham (Site 17). This period has been variously described as the Dark Ages, Post-Roman or **Early Medieval**. The Early Medieval designation continues from the end of the Roman occupation up until the Norman invasion of 1066. During this period South Devon witnessed the arrival of Saxon influence and Alfred the Great established forts, known as *burhs*, throughout his Kingdom; the South Devon location is known as Halwell, and it is disputed as to whether this is Halwell Camp (Site 18) or nearby Stanborough Fort (SX 773516). However, this foundation was short-lived with the *burh* shifting to Totnes (Site 19). The move to Totnes may indicate a pattern of new Saxon foundations protecting the lowest river bridging points from incursions, particularly by Vikings who were now active, with some evidence to suggest that Kingsteignton, Kingsbridge and Plympton were contemporary establishments. It has been suggested that the walls at the enigmatic site of Oldaport, near Modbury (SX635494) are of a Late Saxon *burh* that was added to further protect from Viking attacks as their motive changed from raiding to conquest (see Derek Gore's *The Vikings and Devon*).

The Guide

The Guide is divided by period as described above. The general location of each site is indicated by its number on the map.

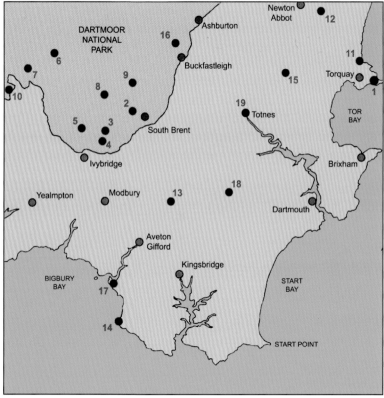

Location of sites listed in this guide. *Reproduced by permission of Ordnance Survey on behalf of HMSO. © Crown Copyright 2010. All rights reserved. Ordnance Survey licence number 100049781.*

Palaeolithic

1. Kents Cavern Prehistoric Habitation Site, Wellswood, Torquay

NGR. SX934642 Web: www.kents-cavern.co.uk. Entrance fee.

The cave system at Kents Cavern is a popular tourist attraction as much for its geological as its archaeological interest. It is one of the most significant sites for the Palaeolithic period in the country. Visit is by guide only.

The cavern is actually a pair of parallel and connecting chambers which reach back some 120 metres in to the Devonian limestone of the hillside. The pair of entrances would have overlooked the dry Ilsham Valley that descends to the coast at Meadfoot Beach. For most of the history of the use of the site the sea would have been replaced by dry land.

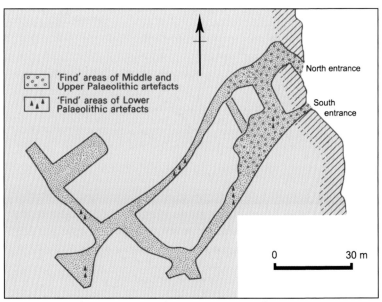

Fig. 4: Plan of Kents Cavern (after Straw 1983)

The major archaeological remains are located near the cave entrances. Early excavations were conducted between 1825 and 1829 by the Rev. John MacEnery of Torre Abbey and were followed by William Pengelly who excavated here between 1865 and 1880. There have been several minor excavations since then. Among the most important finds were hand axes and flakes from a rubble deposit beneath a stalagmite floor, the latter being at least 350,000 years old. Reanalysis of these finds suggests that they may be at least 500,000 years old, which represent some of the earliest evidence of humans in southern Britain. Lower, Middle and Upper Palaeolithic periods are represented by animal remains, flint tools and other artefacts, which may be seen displayed at Torquay Museum.

A jawbone, originally excavated in 1927, has been radiocarbon dated to 40,000 to 35,000 years ago raising the possibility that it may belong to a Neanderthal rather than an archaic human.

Despite the focus of the site being on the rare Palaeolithic remains, artefacts from excavations have yielded evidence that the cave was in use through the Mesolithic and up to the medieval period. It became a show cave in 1880. Kents Cavern should be visited in conjunction with a viewing of the collections on display at the Torquay Museum on Babbacombe Road (www.torquaymuseum.org).

Neolithic

2. Corringdon Ball Long Barrow, Brent Fore Hill, South Brent
NGR: SX669614

This long barrow takes its name from the distinct rounded hill rising to its south, but itself is situated in a saddle between Corringdon Ball and Brent Fore Hill. Approached from the east or west the barrow presents a distinctive profile standing out in the landscape and typical of long barrows elsewhere in southern Britain. However, approached from other directions the site is at first difficult to spot.

Fig 5: Plan of Corringdon Ball Long Barrow (after Butler 1993)

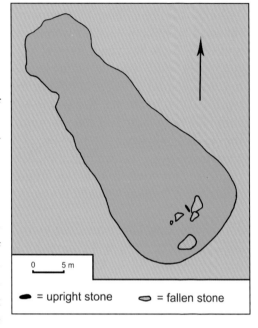

The megalithic burial chamber end of the barrow, which now consists of a tumble of stones, some presumably lost to the field wall nearby, is at the south-east of the

● = upright stone   ◌ = fallen stone

barrow facing Corringdon Ball. Behind the chamber tracking in a north-westerly direction is what remains of the long mound measuring 42 metres in length and 18 metres at its maximum width and still standing to a height of 2.4 m. The mound has been truncated by a track crossing in front of the tail. There is no record of excavation at the site.

Nearby to the west, and visible across the Glaze Brook, are the remains of a complex of stone rows and related cairn circle, which are interesting to visit. The remains, made of small stones, are supposed to represent a single row and two triple rows which end in the remains of a cairn circle (the remains of kerb stones surrounding a burial cairn). These will likely have been constructed many millennia after the long barrow during the Bronze Age.

12

Fig 6: Corringdon Ball Long Barrow

3. Cuckoo Ball Long Cairn, Ugborough
NGR: SX659582

The area of Dartmoor around Butterdon Hill and up to Three Barrows (Site 8) is extremely rich in prehistoric archaeology, with several Bronze Age cairns and stone rows to be observed. It also possess two of the rare (perhaps six known within Dartmoor National Park) burial mounds of the early Neolithic. These are of the same general type as the Corringdon Ball Long Barrow, but are named Long Cairns in acknowledgement that the mounds appear to be made mostly of stones rather than the earthen version at Corringdon Ball.

Although often regarded as the finest dolmen ruin on Dartmoor the site of Cuckoo Ball is actually the most disturbed and despite the clarity of the stone chamber remains the cairn itself has been

Fig 7: Plan of Cuckoo Ball Long Cairn (after Butler 1993)

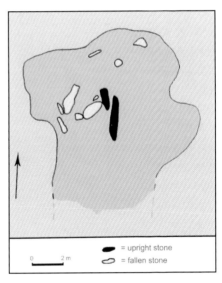

= upright stone
= fallen stone

much denuded for stone for the walls to the west and north. It appears that the chamber sits at the north end of the long cairn which may be traced for 23 metres to the south, with a width of 12 metres and maximum height of 0.7 metres. In essence the Long Cairn faces up hill and if contemporary vegetation allowed people approaching the entrance would be treated to superb views of South Devon.

Fig 8: Cuckoo Ball Long Cairn

4. Butterdon Hill Long Cairn, Ugborough
NGR: SX660586

Some 400 metres northeast of Cuckoo Ball is Butterdon Hill Cairn. This may be difficult to locate when the vegetation is high as its construction appears not to have been on the monumental scale of Cuckoo Ball and today stands to a maximum height of 0.7 metres. What it lacks in height in comparison to Cuckoo Ball it makes up for in the integrity of the long mound which is on a north to south orientation and measures 23 metres in length and 12.5 metres in width, providing a plan wider at the uphill burial chamber end and narrowing at the lower tail. Several stones stand upright forming a north-south line east of centre and it is tempting to propose that these formed the side walls of a long chamber emanating from the northern entrance.

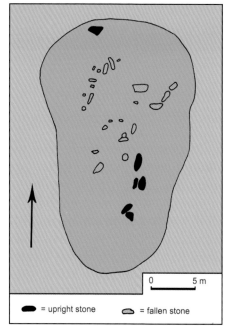

= upright stone   ◠ = fallen stone

Fig 9: Plan of Butterdon Hill Long Cairn (after Fletcher, Grinsell and Quinnell 1974)

Alternatively, they may have formed part of a secondary lateral chamber that is found in this type of monument elsewhere, with an entrance from the side of the mound. What is certain, unless much stone has been removed, is that the height of any chamber will be comparatively low and difficult of access. Neither Cuckoo Ball nor

15

this site has been subjected to archaeological excavation.

Fig 10: Butterdon Hill Long Cairn

5. Stone Row and Cairns, Stalldown Barrow, Cornwood
NGR: SX633623

The tall stones and location of this stone row which crests the ridge of Stalldown Barrow makes it one of the most spectacular on Dartmoor. Approached from the south it gives a sense of drawing one on to the high moor with the most northerly of standing pillars being the tallest standing up to 2.5 metres high. Two further stones lie recumbent beyond these and likely formed part of the row. Several burial monuments are located on Stalldown Barrow, the most obvious of which is the large cairn of Hilson's House east of the stone row (SX637623) in which a much more recent small shelter has been built. Between the north end of the stone row and Hilson's House is an excellent example of ring cairn, at some 24 metres across, this is marked as an 'enclosure' on earlier maps, directly adjacent on its west side is a small cairn of more typical type.

Fig 11: Stalldown row and incorporated cairn

The stone row is some 500 metres long, although Butler proposes a southerly extension, which might have some merit, of a further 340 metres. A cairn appears to have been built into the row some three-quarters of a way along its length. Its current form is of the kerb circle with the majority of cairn material removed. It was excavated in the 1890s by Reverend Sabine Baring-Gould at the same time as the stone row was restored – an incorrect restoration may be responsible for the apparent misalignment of the row where it meets this cairn. R.H. Worth (1967) states that the north part of the row should be tangential to the cairn and not aligned on it; such an arrangement would form a straight, rather than dog-legged, row.

Fig 12: Stalldown row

Adjacent to the top end of the row stand two cairns, one approximately 20 metres to the west and the other 40 metres to the east. The one to the east is a low mound which has been dug in the centre, that to the west appears to have two rings of upright stones and a slab resting on a smaller stone in the north sector of the outer ring has proportions which may suggest it is the displaced capstone from a burial cist originally located at the centre of the cairn.

The general north-south orientation of the row is comparable to that of the Erme Long Row. Visible from the north end of the Stalldown row, the Erme Long Row is perhaps the longest stone row in the world running for a distance of some 3 kilometres from a stone circle forming the terminal of the southerly end (SX635645).

6. Drizzlecombe Stone Row Complex, Shaugh Prior
NGR: SX592670

The Upper Plym Valley has an extraordinary collection of archaeological remains dating to prehistory and later. On both sides of the valley are well-preserved Bronze Age settlements

such as Whittenknowles and Trowlesworthy, and those on Hentor and Willing Walls warrens, all worth exploring if time allows, but the focus here is on the Bronze Age ritual and burial monuments located in a natural basin close to the river and central to the settlement activity.

Fig 13: Drizzlecombe row 1

At a distance the most obvious feature is the impressive Giant's Basin cairn which lies adjacent to the stone rows. It measures 22 metres in diameter and a maximum of 3 metres high. The centre of the cairn has been excavated to a depth of 1.65 metres making a basin shape of the mound. On the west side of the mound are four small cairns (marked I on the plan). There are several other larger cairns in the vicinity (A-H), with three (B-D) marking the upper ends of the stone rows. R.H. Worth proposed that a fourth row was planned between cairn A and a solitary standing stone in the southwest (marked Worth's

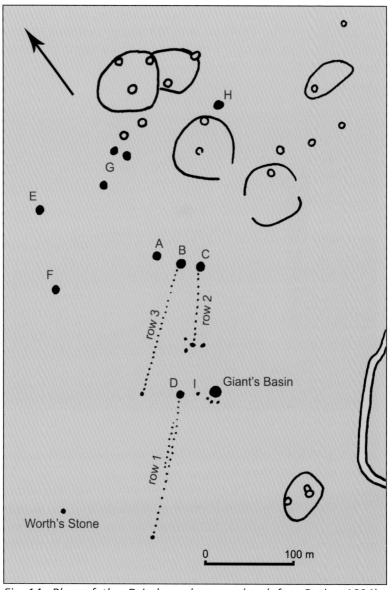

Fig 14: Plan of the Drizzlecombe complex (after Butler 1994)

Stone on the plan). This would have been double the length of the remaining longest row, but would have run parallel to row 3 and, as such, the observation has much to commend it. The rows were restored in the summer of 1893 and at their lower ends are marked by tall standing stones. Cairn E, although out of sight of cairns (A-C) is sited on a similar contour and contains a well-preserved kistvaen (stone box) burial chamber. Excavated by Worth in 1900 it contained no finds.

Fig 15: Drizzlecombe Cairn E

Cairn H at some 20 metres in diameter and 2 metres in height is not much smaller than Giant's Basin cairn. In the present day it appears peculiarly detached from the central complex by having had a settlement enclosure constructed below it in prehistory. It is interesting to note that, according to current convention, several settlement enclosures and round houses were constructed on this hillside after the ritual monuments, but appear to have respected the earlier structures by not cannibalising them for convenient quarries. The neat chronological distinction is somewhat challenged by the group marked G on the plan which take the form of half houses/cairns and presumably were houses before being reused as cairns.

Fig 16: Drizzlecombe row 2

It has been found elsewhere in southern Britain that houses have been turned into cairns at the ends of their or their occupant's lives.

Row 1 has a length of 139.5 metres. The row comprises some ninety stones of which half are doubled which commences about half-way along and runs towards the cairn. The cairn (D) has a number of edge set kerb stones around the circumference of the mound. The standing stone at the opposite end measures 3.2 metres high. Row 2 is the shortest and is 77 metres long. There are fourteen stones in a single row; three of these are fallen with a maximum height for any stone of 0.8 metres. The standing stone at 4.3 metres high is the tallest and is unique at Drizzlecombe in being orientated across the row instead of the widest side being in line with the row. The terminal cairn (C) has ten stones of the retaining kerb circle at the base of the mound. Row 3 is 146 metres long and there are

69 upright stones and 2 fallen. The terminal standing stone 2.4 metres high. At the opposite end the cairn (B) has a depression in the centre, possibly the site of a kistvaen, and 7 stones of the kerb circle are present.

7. Brisworthy Stone Circle, Brisworthy, Sheepstor
NGR: SX564654

This free-standing stone circle, one of 14 known on Dartmoor, is relatively easy to access and approached from the west has the dramatic backdrop of Legis Tor to enhance it. The tallest stone is 1.4 metres high and there are 25 stones making up this slightly ovoid circle. It was restored in 1909 by Hugh Breton and R.H. Worth. Aubrey Burl (1976) suggested that the community using this circle resided in the large Bronze Age settlement below Legis Tor on the side of the Upper Plym Valley, but without more

Fig 17: Brisworthy Stone Circle

satisfactory dating evidence this can only be speculation, and current orthodoxy would have the circle built several centuries prior to the settlement of round houses.

The purpose of such stone circles, free-standing and unattached to stone rows, of which there are several on Dartmoor, is still the subject of much discussion. Astronomical alignments are often proposed and it is interesting to note at Brisworthy that the tallest stone marks the north. The works of 1909 revealed a great deal of charcoal indicating fires have often been lit within the circle, perhaps providing the focus of certain rituals. The distribution of the free-standing circles on Dartmoor led John Barnatt (1989) to propose that they acted as early markers of community territories later replaced by the watershed reaves, such as found at Three Barrows (see Site 8).

Bronze Age

8. Three Barrows Cairns and Reave, Ugborough Moor
NGR: SX654626

The central cairn occupying the summit of this hill is one of the largest on Dartmoor and measures 45 metres northwest-southeast by 38 metres southwest-northeast and stands up to 2.5 metres high. It has a slightly concave top and has evidently been disturbed since construction and the diameter of the cairn has no doubt spread as a result. To the northwest and southeast are smaller cairns making up the Three Barrows of the hill. Of these, that on the south-east has survived best measuring 22 metres in diameter and 1.5 metres high and has spread to connect with a large boundary reave on its western side. The cairn in the northwest measures 22 metres in diameter and up to 1.4 metres high. It was devastated by excavation in the nineteenth century with no finds reported, although there were some indications of stone lined pits, presumably for burials, of which there is no longer any obvious evidence. From certain points north of the hill this cairn located on the shoulder of the hill looks more prominent than the higher central cairn. To the west and south-west of the cairn are many small quarry pits that may have been used to supply the stone for the three cairns, but R.H. Worth noted that they were made to supply stone for the Redlake Railway construction below the hill to the west. The angular nature of the majority of the stones forming the cairns suggest that they have not been brought from the valley bottoms, but they could be as equally derived from surface collection as from quarrying.

Fig 18: Three Barrows central cairn from northwest cairn

The reave climbs the hill from the southwest and makes for the central cairn and on the other side continues out north. The size of this reave is impressive having a breadth of 3 metres in places and a form which makes it understandable that earlier antiquaries regarded it as the remains of a trackway. In the early twentieth century William Crossing (1912) noted in his guide to Dartmoor that the reave at Three Barrows could not possibly be

Fig 19: Three Barrows quarry pits

a trackway as it was slighted by two of the three cairns. Following the systematic research of Andrew Fleming (2008) we now know this reave as a 'watershed reave' built as a boundary to separate the territories of neighbouring groups - another fine example of this type of reave can be seen associated with the cairn on Pupers Hill (SX675674). As with stone circles (see Site 7) the large hilltop cairns, of which over 100 are known on Dartmoor, may have served as markers of territories, prior to the construction of the watershed reaves. Other reaves form the boundaries of fields, such as at Saddlesborough (Site 10).

9. Rider's Rings Prehistoric Settlement, Shipley Bridge, South Brent
NGR: SX679644

Although less restored, the Bronze Age settlement of Rider's (Ryder's) Rings on the eastern slope of Zeal Plains, is certainly the equal of the better known Grimspound on eastern Dartmoor (SX700809). It is formed by two connected enclosures, the most southerly of which is regarded as the first built, and together enclose an area of approximately 2.8 hectares (7 acres) making it one of the largest on Dartmoor. The settlement encloses 26 house circles and some 25 or 26 sub-rectangular walled areas which, being too large to have been roofed, have been variously termed pens, courts or yards. The enclosure wall has spread but is still impressive and its original thickness averages approximately 2.4 metres. The construction seems to have been an inner and outer face with a rubble core.

Fig 20: Rider's Rings enclosure wall

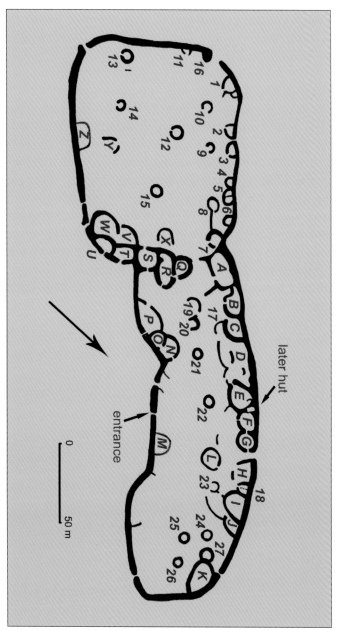

Fig 21: Plan of Rider's Rings (after Butler 1993)

In August 1930 R.H. Worth excavated two house circles in the northern enclosure and examined the perimeter wall. Yards I and L were also trenched and no reported finds support the interpretation of their use as animal pens. House circle 18 was cleared revealing a hearth with a stone fire-screen, still standing, protecting the fire from wind gusting through the southeast facing door. Finds included pottery fragments, flint flakes, cooking stones and charcoal. Hemery (1986) reports that a further 14 huts were excavated in 1936 by the Devon Archaeological Exploration Society who found "sundry items of domestic ware [and] a four-inch whetstone".

The house circles are found in both enclosures and are either attached to the interior of the perimeter wall or free-standing. There are several good examples and the majority have entrances orientated to the south-east with views down the Avon Valley. In contrast to the slab built versions found elsewhere on Dartmoor the smaller stones available locally have been used to build several wall courses; a good example of this can be seen in the interior wall of house circle 12. House circle 1 has a door jamb standing and appears to have an attached annexe to its north. Such annexes to houses are quite common on Dartmoor, and one excavated across the Avon Valley on Hickaton Hill was found to enclose a storage pit dug into the granite bed rock (Fox 1957). From the north end of Rider's Rings the Hickaton Hill prehistoric settlements are visible. The lowest of these, semi-submerged in the waters of the reservoir, was extensively excavated by Lady Fox over three seasons from 1954-56 and in generalities may shed some light on the house circles at Rider's Rings. Fox's findings showed that the conical roofs of the houses were supported by a central pole and interior ring of posts a metre or so inside the wall. The entrances were paved continuing a little way inside and out of the house, and on occasions a sleeping area could be defined at the rear of the house. The placement of the hearth was apparently a matter of personal preference, and there were often pits perhaps as soak-aways, cooking pits or pot stands close to the hearths in most houses. A unique find was that of a bead of smelted tin, which is a key indicator that the occupants of the settlements in the Dartmoor valleys were exploiting the tin deposits – a necessary component (with copper) of bronze.

Fig 22: Rider's Rings house circle

It has often been commented that there is much space available within the enclosures for the corralling of animals, but we need to remember, as illustrated by excavations elsewhere on the moor, that there may have been several buildings constructed of wood which do not survive as upstanding remains; an indication of this may be revealed by the peculiar dog leg in the wall of Yard B forming enough space for a wooden house circle between it and Yard A.

Several gaps in the enclosure wall have been suggested as original entrances, but only one appears as indisputably original. This is located facing southeast midway along the downhill wall of the northerly enclosure. It is only 0.7 metres wide and is well made with tidy finishing of the wall ends on either side of the passage. There has been debate about the form of entrances into the prehistoric enclosures of Dartmoor, particularly since the complete excavation of Site 15 on Shaugh Moor failed to locate one, and this diminutive entrance, wide enough for cattle to pass only in single file, may be more typical than the more difficult to close and control reconstruction at Grimspound.

The yards which are a feature of this site are known from other Dartmoor enclosures and suit the interpretation that the Bronze Age settlements of southwest Dartmoor were built by communities with a largely pastoral economy where sheep and cattle were grazed on the high moors and regularly brought in overnight to protect them from predators and rustlers. This compares to the crop-based communities of southeast Dartmoor with their extensive field systems. Evidence of domestic animals comes from proxy sources as bones do not survive in the acid soils of the moorland (see Saddlesborough Site 10 below for an example of such evidence).

10. Saddlesborough Prehistoric Field System, Settlements and Stone Settings, Shaugh Moor, Shaugh Prior
NGR: SX553635

The gentle west and north-facing slopes of Saddlesborough contain a rich and easily accessible assortment of Late Neolithic and Bronze Age archaeology. The archaeological remains consist of an extensive field system with associated settlement sites on the western slope and to the north of this beyond the Saddlesborough Terminal Reave further well-preserved settlement remains and ceremonial and burial monuments. The

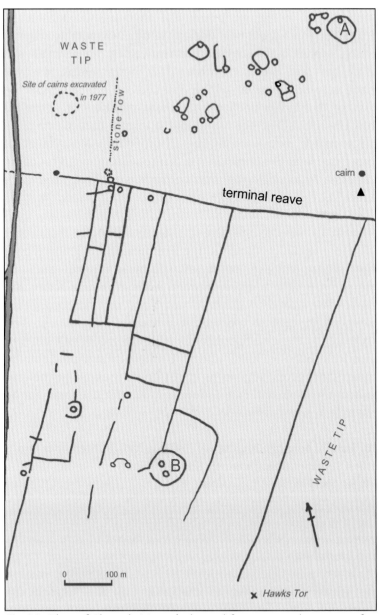

WASTE
TIP

Site of cairns excavated
in 1977

stone row

cairn ●

▲

terminal reave

WASTE TIP

A

B

0   100 m

✕ Hawks Tor

Fig 23: Plan of Shaugh Moor (adapted from several sources after the original plan by J. Collis, 1978 and 1983)

Saddlesborough Terminal Reave is a prehistoric field boundary which appears to separate this portion of prehistoric landscape, which is surrounded by improved land in the west and south and china clay quarrying in the north and east. The terminal reave has the role of providing the orientation for the co-axial field

Fig 24:
Saddlesborough stone row

system which runs in a block system to its south. Over a dozen fields can be discerned by the surviving low stone banks and lynchets. Next to the terminal reave, where the fields appear to be more tightly clustered than is otherwise the case, is a collection of 4 house circles, 3 to the south of the reave and one adjacent and north of the reave. The one north of the reave is adjacent to a stone circle some 12 metres in diameter and defined by 6 small stones which remain of its circuit with perhaps two missing. Directly north of the circle is a stone row, heading north for approximately 173 metres. Approximately halfway along the row and to its east is the denuded remains of kerbed burial cairn, which has often been confused as the remains of a house circle - the location next to the row confirms the likely burial function of these remains. To the west of the row, now buried under the spoil of china clay quarrying was the site of several cairns excavated in 1977. The excavation revealed a small Bronze Age ring cairn with a central pit containing the base of a pottery vessel and seven rare faience beads; faience is a mix of clay and sand highly fired so that the surface turns to a bluish or greenish glass. Such finds are more typical of the Wessex area of southern Britain, but the nearby china clay would have been suitable raw material for such beads and may indicate that beads of this type were being manufactured locally. The remains of a further kerb cairn can be seen closer to the road, the proximity to which appears to account for its damage as a useful quarry for road menders/builders.

The Saddlesborough Terminal Reave was once far more extensive extending to the east across the area now occupied by the huge china clay extraction operations, it also extended west

Fig 25:
Saddlesborough
terminal reave

and can be seen continued in the more recent field boundary across the road on the facing shallow valley side. In the big plan of things it appears then to turn north-eastwards and connects to the reave which climbs to the summit of

34

Eylesbarrow (SX599686). Part of Saddlesborough reave was excavated in the late 1970s ahead of expansion of the china clay works and showed that a fence and ditch had likely preceded the stone-built reave. In the ditch was found a mass of hoof prints representing cow and sheep with a few of horse. This was an excellent indication of the animals being farmed, as bones do not survive in the acid upland soils. Along with pollen analysis indicating the cultivation of cereals and beans, the findings provided a picture of mixed farming in a landscape still being opened up in the middle Bronze Age. A plaster cast of the hoof prints may be examined in the archaeology display at Plymouth City Museum and Art Gallery.

The Saddlesborough Terminal Reave does not cross the summit of Saddlesborough Hill, but traverses just to the south. On the summit close to the triangulation point marker is reportedly the remains of at least three cairns, but there has been much disturbance by quarrying and the clearest is adjacent to and south of the outcrop north of the triangulation point. It is visible as a circular rim approximately 2.5 metres wide and some 18 metres in diameter.

The north facing slope below the triangulation point has a series Bronze Age house circles and enclosures. The furthest north (marked A on the plan) has a single house circle. Further north, in the area covered by the china clay works a complete enclosure (named Site 15) was excavated in 1977 and 1978. Interestingly, it was found that the houses had been built first with the enclosure wall added at a later date a situation which is apparent at A where the enclosure was evidently built to incorporate the house circle in its circuit. Site 15 showed that settlement occurred over a very long period, perhaps up to a 1000 years and into the early Iron Age, and that several structures in the enclosure were of wooden construction, something that should be borne in mind when looking at the obvious stone remains on the slopes of

Saddlesborough. Another telling finding from Site 15 was the apparent lack of an entrance to the enclosure, with the excavators suggesting that a stile type structure may have been used to enter the settlement. Next to Enclosure A are three house circles partly connected by a low wall, the northernmost house has door jambs in place facing southwest.

Fig 26: Saddlesborough house circle doorway

Crossing to the south of the Saddlesborough Terminal Reave the coaxial field system strikes down the hillside and within it are several settlement sites, the most impressive of which is marked B on the plan. Here the enclosure is defined by a substantial stone and turf bank lined with large orthostats in the interior and sloping externally. The latter feature is likely a later modification for stock corralling as it is not typical of prehistoric construction, and this is undoubtedly a prehistoric enclosure with two clearly defined house circles within and a reave abutting it to the north. The reave approaching from the north and the field boundary to the north and east has some impressive orthostats in their construction. Despite the assertions of other commentators there is no clear evidence that the enclosure was built astride the already existing reave and an opposite chronology of enclosure first followed by the field system appears to suit the extant remains. The breaks in the enclosure wall all appear to be recent, but there may be an indication of an earlier entrance, now blocked, in the western side where two slabs of stone approximately 1.5 metres apart sit transverse to the wall.

Fig 27: Saddlesborough enclosure B

The peculiar metal poles with stars on top were erected by the Ministry of Public Buildings and Works in the late 1960s when Shaugh Moor was used as military training ground to warn of archaeological sites and may, where they still stand, be used to locate the remains.

Dartmoor is deservedly famous for the survival of its prehistoric field systems, but another survival in South Devon should be noted here, it is on the coast at **Decklers Cliff** (SX758367) and occupies an area of approximately 11 hectares on a very steep north-facing slope. Here lynchets form well-proportioned rectilinear fields with at least 36 fields identified. The lynchets are anything up to 2.0m high and a number have low, spread earthen banks or a line of short upright slabs of local stone along their top edges. Some of the lynchets link areas of outcropping rock. The lynchets are likely formed by later ploughing within the prehistoric field system. Two house circles have been identified within the system.

Fig 28: Decklers Cliff

11. Walls Hill Prehistoric Field System, Babbacombe, Torquay
NGR: SX934650

The walls of Walls Hill are an impressive survival of what is often termed in the literature as 'Celtic fields'. That is a collection of relatively small fields related to early farming. In South Devon there are several survivals to be found on the light soils overlying limestone geology (Gallant, Luxton and Collman 1985). Perhaps the best known was that which existed at Dainton (SX859668), where several excavations of field boundaries and associated clearance cairns ahead of the expansion of Stoneycombe Quarry uncovered finds of late Bronze Age and Iron Age date, including moulds for casting bronze spearheads and swords.

Fig 29: Walls Hill field boundary

The remains at Walls Hill are located on a cliff top promontory overlooking Anstey's Cove to the south. Cliff top erosion indicates that the field system probably originally extended further to the south and there are remains of cairns and bank to the north to indicate that it extended further in this direction also. To the southwest a quarry has probably further truncated the pattern of fields. The area now extant is approximately 5 hectares and easily accessible across the park from the Babbacombe side.

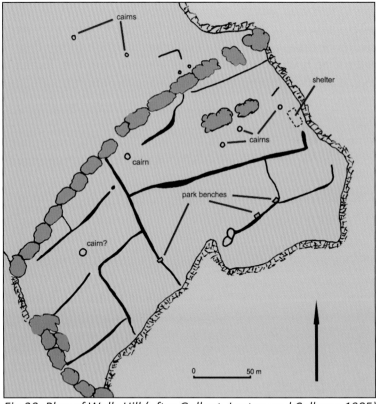

Fig 30: Plan of Walls Hill (after Gallant, Luxton and Collman 1985)

The Walls Hill remains are similar to those excavated at Dainton, although not all of the cairns should be dismissed simply as 'clearance cairns' as some of these are quite large (up to 11 metres in diameter) and that marked with a question mark on the plan has a form which may represent a ring cairn or even a house circle. Many of the cairns were opened by antiquarians and these were followed by Reverend MacEnery of Kents Cavern fame who excavated some of the 'maiden' cairns in 1825, although only one contained finds of note, including fragments of pottery. MacEnery was of the opinion that the remains dated to the Roman period. The banks are best defined on the south side where they survive to a height of up to 0. 4 metres and 4 to 5 metres in width. Some of the lynchetting is likely the result of ploughing known to have taken place on the site in the eighteenth century.

12. Milber Down Hill-Slope Fort, Coffinswell, Newton Abbot
NGR: SX883698

Despite being dissected by a major road the banks and ditches at Milber Down preserve well the outline of three inner enclosures and to a lesser extent a fourth outer enclosure of a hill-slope fort typical of the Iron Age in Southwest England. The banks and ditches of the inner enclosures are of a similar nature and vary in height of bank from 0.5 to 1.5 metres and in depth of ditch from 0.5 to 2.0 metres. The entrance to the fort faced northwest with the modern road following the entrance through the three inner enclosures. Beyond the third enclosure an entrance passage, flanked by banks and ditches, doglegs to the north and back to the northwest where it meets the remnants of the outer enclosure.

Small-scale investigations in 1937-1938 found curvilinear decorated pottery, similarly decorated spindle whorls for spinning woollen thread and evidence of clay ovens indicated that the site was settled beginning 2,400 years ago. Three small figurines of bronze were recovered during the excavations. They depict a duck, with a disc in its mouth, a stag in repose and a bird with a long tail. The objects came from the ditch of the second enclosure. The collection was placed in the top of the fill of the ditch and may have been deposited close to the end of the use of the site at around 50 to 55 AD. They are held at Torquay Museum.

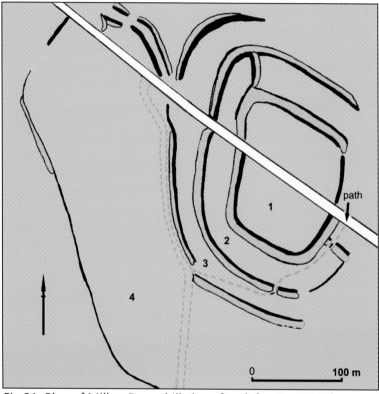

Fig 31: Plan of Milber Down hill-slope fort (after Fox 1987)

Beyond the fourth enclosure above the fort has been located the remains of a probable Romano-British farmstead which may have superseded the fort.

13. Blackdown Rings Hillfort, Loddiswell
NGR: SX720520

Situated on the south side of a hill top at 185 metres above sea level and commanding the Avon Valley to the east stands the impressive earthworks of the Blackdown Rings (sometimes Loddiswell Rings or just 'The Rings'). The Iron Age hillfort consisted of a single rampart and ditch with evidence, particularly in the southeast, of a further (counterscarp) bank on the outside edge of the ditch. The rampart stands to a height of 1.7 metres with the ditch reaching 2 metres in depth. The hillfort enclosed an area of 2 hectares. In the Norman period a motte and bailey type castle was inserted within the northwest corner of the castle and the hillfort appears to have been further modified to provide an outer enclosure for the castle.

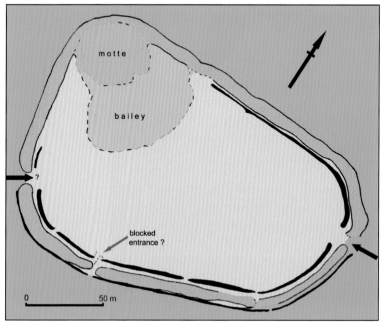

Fig 32: Plan of Blackdown Rings (based on drawing in Wilson-North and Dunn 1990, ©Crown copyright. NMR)

An original entrance to the hillfort appears to be the eastern gap which, although widened in modern times, retains an in-turned rampart and ditch on the north side, the south having been truncated. The western entrance is a simple gap, widened in modern times and may be related to the Norman modifications. Southeast of this entrance may be the remains of an original Iron Age gateway which has been blocked in antiquity; this is suggested by the gap in rampart here and the well-defined causeway 4 metres wide which crosses the ditch at this point. The interior has been ploughed in living memory and there are no features of note. The location commands superb views to the east and west and the motte (which may be better described as a ringwork) appears historically to have served as a beacon platform.

Fig 33:
Blackdown
Rings ditch

14. Bolt Tail Promontory Fort, Hope Cove, South Huish
NGR: SX668397

Bolt Tail is a promontory of steep-sided cliff forming the southeastern limit of Bigbury Bay. It provides shelter for the small sandy bay of Hope Cove. The headland is separated from the rest of the coastal lands by a steep-sided dry valley running southwest to northeast and probably following the line of a geological fault. On its northwest side the top of the valley has been utilised for the enhancement of a single rampart and ditch defining an area of approximately 6 hectares within. This type of site is commonly termed a 'promontory fort' or 'cliff castle' and is more typical of the Atlantic coasts of the southwest peninsula and usually dated to the Iron Age. Another example in South Devon may have been on the very high cliffs of Berry Head overlooking Tor Bay (SX945565); the 'Berry' name being suggestive and the ditch being re-used by the Napoleonic-era fort, but this is by no means proven.

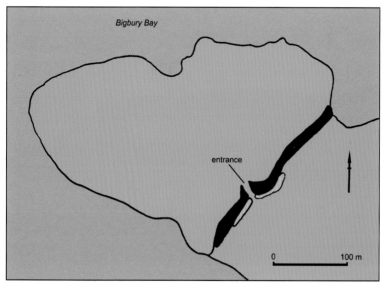

Fig 34: Plan of Bolt Tail (after Quinnell 1992)

The earthwork consists of a rampart 275 metres long and up to 4.6 metres high, with indications of a stone facing wall over 1 metre high on its outer eastern side towards the northern end. The original entrance appears to be central to the rampart, although it is likely that erosion has shortened the earthwork where it meets the cliff edges. A hollow-way enters through an in-turned entrance quite typical of Iron Age fortifications, and it appears that a natural outcrop has been incorporated on the north side to add further height and solidity to the entrance works. Later ploughing has removed much of the features external to the fort, but remnants of the ditch can still be seen to either side of the entrance.

Griffith and Wilkes (2006) make the interesting observation that the oblique direction of the entrance through the rampart means that any visitor, supposing there were no structures to

Fig 35: View of Bolt Tail

Fig 36: Bolt Tail entrance

disrupt the view, would be directed to a vista incorporating a view filled centrally by Burgh Island located across Bigbury Bay. Burgh Island together with Mount Batten next to Sutton Harbour, Plymouth, St. Michael's Mount in Mount's Bay, Cornwall and the Isle of Wight, is one of the proposed identifications for the *Ictis* of antiquity. This was a place described by Diodorus Siculus, writing 2000 years ago, as an island lying off the coast of Britain separated by a causeway that dried at low water, where tin was to be traded by the locals with visiting merchants. The view from the fort's gateway to the island may indicate that there was a strong connection between the sites and the people using them in the Iron Age. Brent Hill (SX704617), a later beacon location near South Brent and topped by a rampart of likely Iron Age date, is also visible from the site. Bolt Tail has not been excavated and no surface indication has been recognised showing the presence of internal settlement.

15. Denbury Camp Hillfort, Denbury
NGR: SX817685

The distinctive tree-capped hill of Denbury Camp is a major landmark in South Devon. The morphology of the hillfort indicates that it may have been constructed in two phases. The first phase is an ovoid shaped enclosure defined by a ditch and remnants of a rampart with a further rampart up to 3.5 metres high in the south and east. The earthworks enclose an area of approximately 2 hectares. At a later date in the Iron Age an annexe was added to the west end of the original fort and is defined by a bank up to 3.5 metres high, but apparently ploughed away in the north; later farming activity has created several lynchet type features which have modified the original form of the Camp's earthworks. The Phase 1 fort appears to have had a single entrance which is the in-turned western gap in the earthworks. The annexe entrance is directly south of this, almost where the extension meets the original fort on the south perimeter. Survivals from earlier periods appear to be the two mounds enclosed within the main fort which are probably Bronze Age cairns; originally round, their shape has been distorted by ploughing. These cairns were likely constructed over the burials of important individuals and indicate that the constructors of the fort respected these monuments built a thousand years earlier. The westernmost cairn stands 2 metres high and is 30 metres in diameter. The eastern is ovoid in plan with a maximum diameter of 39 metres and standing 2.5 metres high. Prior to the tree planting on the hilltop the site would have enjoyed extensive views in all directions, which probably accounts for historical reports of a fire beacon here.

The name Denbury has been generally considered as derived from the Old English meaning the 'the fort of the men of Devon'. Such a designation has led to suggestions that this is where the Saxon advance in Devon met strong resistance, but without excavation, and with no stray finds reported to date this remains only conjecture.

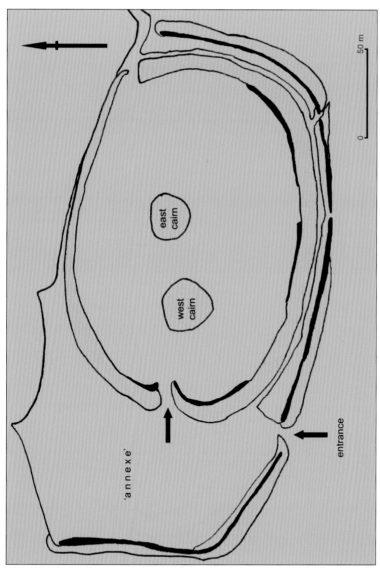

Fig 37: Plan of Denbury Camp (based on drawing in Probert and Dunn 1992, ©Crown copyright. NMR)

16. Hembury Castle Hillfort, Buckfastleigh
NGR: SX726685

The hillfort at Hembury Castle is located on a hill high above the River Dart. It is set in thinned woodland managed by the National

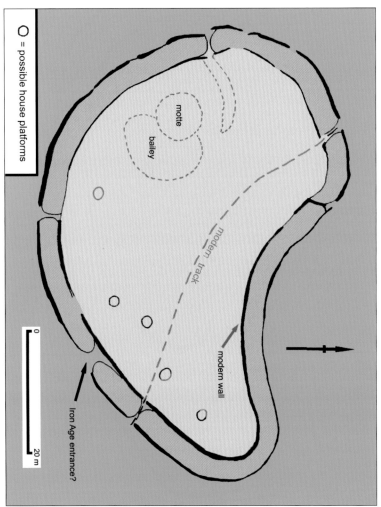

Fig 38: Plan of Hembury Castle hillfort (based on drawing in Timms 1999, ©Crown copyright. NMR)

Trust and is very popular with dog walkers. The visible earthworks are of the original Iron Age fort with a medieval motte and bailey castle inserted at the higher western end. The inner rampart of the Iron Age fort, which once undoubtedly existed, has been levelled and replaced in most sectors by a modern field wall, and today the Iron Age perimeter is marked by the substantial ditch and outer counterscarp mound. The original entrance appears to be in the south-east; the gap now blocked by a modern wall can be seen to break the circuit with a simple entrance and wide causeway across the ditch. Timms (1999) suggests that it is no accident that the entrance faces downhill in the direction of the River Dart where water and other resources could be sourced. In the south-east sector of the fort four or five circular house platforms have been recorded by survey work. The earthworks enclose an area of approximately 7 hectares (17 acres). There are several causeways across the ditch suggesting that either the fort was unfinished or that sections of the ditch were deepened after earlier cutting.

Early Medieval

17. Bantham Ham Trading Settlement, Thurlestone
NGR: SX663438

As far as the archaeology is concerned there is little to see, but a visit to Bantham is a pleasure in itself and the wide surf sprayed beach actively conspires to produce imaginings of traders bringing their boats and goods ashore from the Iron Age, through the Roman and into the early medieval era. The archaeological remains have been exposed through several instances of accidental erosion and planned archaeological investigation. Most well-known are the artefacts relating to a trading settlement of the fifth to seventh centuries AD which included imported jars and amphorae from the Mediterranean - similar finds are noted further west along the coast at Mothecombe (SX611474).

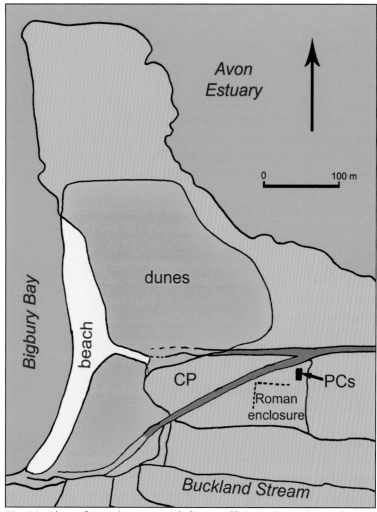

Fig 39: Plan of Bantham Ham (after Griffith and Reed 1998)

The whole area under the sand dunes appears to hide potential archaeological information. Excavations at the south end in 2001 found hearths and much evidence of feasting on a wide variety of domestic and wild animals including beef, pork, mutton, venison, rabbit, duck and chicken and sherds of amphora suggesting that Byzantine wine was used to wash it down. Such finds support reports that in about 1900 cartloads of bone was taken from Bantham and used to fertilise the fields. In 1997 an excavation ahead of toilet block construction revealed unsuspected remains of a substantial late-Roman period stone-revetted enclosure of at least 50 metres in length (Griffith and Reed 1998). Though the site is now reburied it revealed that a great deal more is likely still to be discovered here.

18. Halwell Camp, Halwell
NGR: SX784532

On the hill above the village of Halwell and bisected by the road to Dartmouth is a sub-circular earthwork enclosure. Where the road crosses the fort is a lay-by which allows easy parking to visit the site which may be one of great historic importance. The late Saxon Burghal Hidage of circa 918 AD records the location of four forts, known as *burhs*, in Devon of which one, listed as Hacganwille is translated as 'the *burh* at Halwell'. Established by King Alfred, these *burhs* were constructed as part of a system to defend the Kingdom of Wessex from Viking incursions. Later monarchs re-organised and enhanced the system and this *burh* was replaced by one at Totnes (see Site 19 below). The site today is best preserved to the north, where, at the time of writing access is allowed, and consists of a single rampart standing to 2.6 metres high with evidence of an external ditch. What appears to be a simple single entrance facing north is probably recent and the modern road may have taken route of least resistance through the original entrance (as at Milber Down, Site 12). The enclosure is about 80 metres in diameter and there is nothing to reveal any historic associations. In style and location, given that like others in the region it is located below the crown of the hill, it would best suit the description of an Iron Age fort.

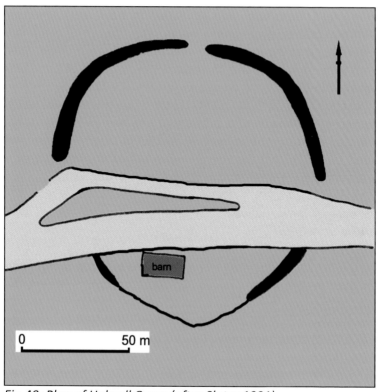

Fig 40: Plan of Halwell Camp (after Slater 1991)

The summit of the hill is to the north of the fort and commands a much better vista from north-west to south-east, including the likely beacon sites of Brent Hill and Beacon Hill above Paignton (with TV and radio masts). Located here is an impressive Bronze Age barrow. Standing today some 3 metres in height and 24 metres in diameter this earthen barrow is the best surviving of 4 barrows once situated on this hilltop, Bickleigh Brake. The neighbouring hill to the south, upon which is located Stanborough Fort (more about which below) also had a barrow cemetery of up to 11 barrows, known as the

Fig 41: Barrow at Bickleigh Brake

Ritson Group, like the three denuded ones of Bickleigh Brake they have all been sadly reduced by plunder and ploughing. Also now missing is a standing stone, known as the 'Old Man'. The barrows, standing stone, forts and other earthworks in the vicinity indicate that this pair of hills was a major focus of activity in prehistory, and this likely relates to the meeting of two ridgeway tracks which converge at Stanborough Camp; one links Dartmoor and the coast at Slapton and the other crosses the grain of the country west–east. There are also several branches to these tracks nearby adding to the attractiveness of placing a *burh* somewhere in this vicinity (Slater 1991). Others have suggested that Stanborough Fort, although likely Iron Age in origin, would have better suited a site for the *burh*; a claim which is enhanced by the site giving its name to the later Saxon hundred, an administrative district. Unfortunately, there is no public access to the site of Stanborough Fort, but the track to its

Fig 42: Stanborough Fort bank and ditch

east follows the line of the old turnpike road and reveals views of the earthworks of rampart 2 metres high with evidence of stone facing and fronted by a ditch.

Halwell Camp, Stanborough Fort and the other sites in the vicinity have not been subject to modern archaeological excavation.

19. Totnes *Burh*

Although probably not fully describing the complexities of the situation the conventional understanding is that Devon had four royal *burhs*, a system of forts first established in the reign of King Alfred (871-899 AD), located at Barnstaple/Pilton, Lydford, Exeter and Totnes. The fort at Exeter utilised the surviving walls of the defunct Roman town, Lydford appears to have been newly

Fig 43: Aerial Photo of Totnes showing the area covered by the Saxon burh. ©Getmapping.

established, although it may have been the site of an earlier fort, while Barnstaple and Totnes appear to have been secondary choices as estuary-side replacements for hillforts at Pilton and Halwell (Site 18) respectively. The new location on estuaries gave the benefit of controlling communications by bridge and boat when compared to the inland hillfort locations. The advantage in both defence and trade is indicated by the continuing survival of these towns; an estuary location was already chosen for Exeter by the Romans and Lydford, which did not enjoy easy access to the coast, stagnated as a town.

The success of locating Totnes at the head of the Dart estuary means that the surviving Saxon archaeology is likely very limited, but this has been little tested by modern excavation. Watching

briefs and rescue observations have indicated that the town defences were a new build. Evidence for the first minted coin and other historical evidence limit the foundation of Totnes to a period in the late 9th century or early 10th century AD. The rampart was 7 metres in width and up to 5 metres high with a

Fig 44: Totnes East Gate

wood revetted front later replaced by a stone wall 2 metres wide bonded by clay and lime mortar. Close in front of the rampart was a single ditch. This was v-shaped in profile and was very large for this period being approximately 10 metres wide and 5 metres deep.

In Saxon times it is likely that only the west and east gates penetrated the defences with north and south gates added in medieval times. The Saxon town is largely fossilized by the current street plan, and, although this is best appreciated by aerial view. A very good sense of the size of the Saxon settlement can be gained by walking the remains of the circuit and along the central road which is followed by the current High Street.

To follow the northern circuit take the steps on the right signposted the 'rampart walk' while passing up hill through the impressive, but much more recent, East Gate. This takes you around the churchyard to the attractive medieval Guildhall. The church likely stands on or close to the site of the Saxon church and the area of church grounds may be more typical of the size of land allotments (known as *haga*) in the Saxon town, than the long and thin burgage plots running perpendicular from the High street and typical of medieval property division.

The North Gate on Castle Street, just below the Norman castle works, dates to the 12th century, and is located further north (i.e. downhill) than the line of Saxon defences and must indicate a post-Norman adjustment. Rescue excavation on the castle motte has shown that the Saxon ramparts continue beneath it on the northwest side. This location was likely important for long distance signalling through beacon fires as Brent Hill to the west and the Haldon Hills to the north (likely sites of beacon fires) may be seen from here. The south circuit may be traced by following South Street on the line of the in-filled ditch (this in-filling occurred in the early 15th century). The top of South Street, where it meets The Narrows, was likely the site of the West Gate.

Sources

Barnatt, J. 1989 *Stone Circles of Britain.* British Archaeological Reports, 215.

Burl, A. 1976 *The Stone Circles of the British Isles.* Yale University Press.

Butler, J. 1993 *Dartmoor Atlas of Antiquities. Volume 4. The South-East.* Devon Books.

Butler, J. 1994 *Dartmoor Atlas of Antiquities. Volume 3. The South-West.* Devon Books.

Butler, J. 1997 *Dartmoor Atlas of Antiquities. Volume 5. The Second Millennium BC.* Devon Books.

Collis, J. 1978 Fields and settlements on Shaugh Moor, Dartmoor. In H.C. Bowen and P.J. Fowler (eds) *Early Land Allotment in the British Isles.* 23-28. *British Archaeological Reports,* 48.

Collis, J. 1983 Field systems and boundaries on Shaugh Moor and at Wotter, Dartmoor. *Proceedings of the Devon Archaeological Society* 41: 47-61.

Crossing, W. 1965 *Crossing's Guide to Dartmoor.* (B. Le Messurier ed.). David and Charles.

Dyer, M. and Allen, J. 2004 An excavation on the defences of the Anglo-Saxon *burh* and medieval town of Totnes. *Proceedings of the Devon Archaeological Society* 62: 53-78.

Fleming, A. 2008 *The Dartmoor Reaves.* Second Edition. Windgather Press.

Fletcher, M.J., Grinsell, L.V. and Quinnell, N. 1974 A Long Cairn on Butterdon Hill, Ugborough. *Proceedings of the Devon Archaeological Society* 32: 163-165.

Fox, A. 1957 Excavations on Dean Moor, in the Avon Valley, 1954-1956. *Transactions of the Devonshire Association* 89: 18-77.

Fox, A. 1964 *South West England.* Thames and Hudson.

Fox, A. 1987 Milber Down. *Devon Archaeological Society Field Guide*, 1.

Fox, A. 1996 *Prehistoric Hillforts in Devon*. Devon Books.

Gallant, L., Luxton, N. and Collman, M. 1985 Ancient fields on the South Devon limestone plateau. *Proceedings of the Devon Archaeological Society* 43: 23-37.

Gore, D. 2001 *The Vikings and Devon*. Mint Press.

Gore, D. 2006 *Isca – The Fall of Roman Exeter*. Mint Press.

Griffiths, D.M. (ed.) 1994 *The Archaeology of Dartmoor: Perspectives from the 1990s*. Proceedings of the Devon Archaeological Society 52.

Griffith, F.M. 1988 *Devon's Past: An Aerial View*. Devon Books.

Griffith, F.M. and Reed, S.J. 1998 Rescue recording at Bantham Ham, South Devon, in 1997. *Proceedings of the Devon Archaeological Society* 56: 109-131.

Griffith, F.M and Wilkes, E.M. 2006 The land named from the sea? Coastal archaeology and place-names of Bigbury, Devon. *Archaeological Journal* 163: 67-91.

Grinsell, L.V. 1983 The barrows of South and East Devon. *Proceedings of the Devon Archaeological Society* 41: 5-46.

Hemery, E. 1986 *High Dartmoor*. Hale.

Higham, R. 2008 *Making Anglo-Saxon Devon*. Mint Books.

Pearce, S.M. 1981 *The Archaeology of South West Britain*. Collins.

Probert, S.J. and Dunn, C.J. 1992 Denbury Camp, Torbryan Parish: a new survey by the Royal Commission on the Ancient and Historic Monuments of England. *Proceedings of the Devon Archaeological Society* 50: 53-59.

Quinnell, H. 1995 The Drizzlecombe Stone Rows. *Devon Archaeological Society Field Guide*, 11.

Quinnell, N. 1992 Bolt Tail. *Devon Archaeological Society Field Guide*, 8.

Slater, T. 1991 Controlling the South Hams: the Anglo-Saxon *burh* at Halwell. *Transactions of the Devonshire Association* 123: 57-78.

Smith, K., Coppen, J., Wainwright, G.J. and Beckett, S. 1981 The Shaugh Moor Project: third report – settlement and environmental investigations. *Proceedings of the Prehistoric Society* 47: 205-273.

Stansbury, D. 1992 *The Saxon Foundations of Totnes*. Totnes Museum Society.

Straw, A. 1983 Kent's Cavern. *Devon Archaeology* 1: 14-21.

Timms, S. 1999 Hembury Castle, Buckfastleigh. *Devon Archaeological Society Field Guide*, 13.

Todd, M. 1987 *The South-West to AD 1000*. Longman.

Turner, S. and Gerrard, J. 2004 Imported and local pottery from Mothecombe: some new finds amongst old material at Totnes Museum. *Proceedings of the Devon Archaeological Society* 62: 171-175.

Wainwright, G.J., Fleming, A. and Smith, K. 1979 The Shaugh Moor Project – first report. *Proceedings of the Prehistoric Society* 45: 1-33.

Wainwright, G.J. and Smith, K. 1980 The Shaugh Moor Project: second report – the enclosure. *Proceedings of the Prehistoric Society* 46: 65-122.

Wilson-North, W.R. and Dunn, C.J. 1990 'The Rings', Loddiswell: a new survey by the Royal Commission on the Ancient and Historic Monuments of England. *Proceedings of the Devon Archaeological Society* 48: 87-100.

Worth, R.H. 1967 *Worth's Dartmoor*. (G.M. Spooner and F.S. Russell eds) David and Charles.